642

THINGS TO WRITE ABOUT

BY THE SAN FRANCISCO WRITERS' GROTTO

INTRODUCTION BY PO BRONSON

CHRONICLE BOOKS

SAN FRANCISCO

CONTRIBUTORS

Molly Antopol
Tom Barbash
Natalie Baszile
J.D. Beltran
Po Bronson
Xandra Castleton
Marianna Cherry
Chris Colin
Chris Cook
Stephen Elliott
Isaac Fitzgerald
Laura Fraser
Susie Gerhard
Melanie Gideon
Connie Hale
Noah Hawley
Rachel Howard
Gerard Jones

Diana Kapp
Connie Loizos
Kathryn Ma
Jordan Mackay
Anne Marino
Josh McHugh
Ashley Merryman
David Munro
Janis Newman
Peter Orner
Caroline Paul
Jason Roberts
Julia Scheeres
Justine Sharrock
Meghan Ward
Ethan Watters
Matthew Zapruder

Library of Congress Cataloging-in-Publication Data
available.

ISBN: 978-1-4521-0544-4

Manufactured in China.

Designed by Eloise Leigh

20 19 18 17

Chronicle Books LLC
680 Second Street
San Francisco, California 94107
www.chroniclebooks.com

This book was written in a single day. A single 24-hour period, with no advance notice. Nor was it our idea. An editor-friend of mine rang out of the blue and said, "Let's do a book called *642 Things to Write About*."

My gut response was, "Great, but you don't mean *literally* 642 things, right? You're using 642 just to represent any big number, so it could be 238 things or 187 things—I mean, 642 things is going to be kind of impossible."

"Okay, we could do a different number," she said, then paused. "But I *was* thinking 642 things. Literally."

I was not going to tackle this alone. So the next morning, I e-mailed my office mates at the San Francisco Writers' Grotto. There are thirty-five writers here, a warren maze of small offices and library-like carrels. My thought was that if we came up with more than a hundred writing ideas on the first day, then maybe this project could be real. I thought it would take a month.

People started e-mailing in ideas, in bunches. We had a hundred within an hour. Five hundred by the end of the day, and the ideas kept flowing overnight. Contributions came in from thirty-five different writers. At lunchtime the following day, I delivered the finished manuscript, in person, to our editor.

I tell this story because it's a lesson in hidden potential. You never know what might happen. In a single day, if you hit the right nerve, you could have something—maybe it's the start of something, maybe it's the whole thing. And it doesn't even have to begin with your own idea. You just have to get creative and plunge in.

You could use these 642 things literally, by picking an exercise and completing it. Or you can just let them wash over you to stir up your creativity, to remind you that no, not everything has been written, not every good idea is already taken by someone else. There are an infinite number of things one could write about and so many fresh directions for your story to go.

PO BRONSON
San Francisco Writers' Grotto

What can happen in a second

The cold wind rushed through my veins mingling with the adrenaline. I was relieved ... until guilt began seeping in. I hated him. I hated him. I hated him! He deserved it I told myself but I knew it didn't justify what I had done.

Blood sunk into my t-shirt creating a red stain that I knew would never come out but that was the least of my worries. I'm a murderer ...

The worst Thanksgiving dish you ever had

I woke up earlier than usual as I was so excited. I ran downstairs to realise my ~~watch~~ alarm clock was wrong. It turned out that it was actually 4pm which is the latest time I've ever woken up. There was no food left and no shops were open. All I had was a bowl of rice.

It was as bland as flour and almost as dry. I could smell the post dinner on the table and felt jealous as I reluctantly at my rice.

A houseplant is dying. Tell it why it needs to live.

You can't die on me! Your luxious, vibrant green leaves shine in the sunlight. You've grown to be so perfect and I've never seen any plant as beautiful as you in a pot. Have you heard the compliments people have said and the jealous looks. Any plant would be lucky to be anything like you. This is why you can't die — you make me so happy in the mornings when I water you.

Write Facebook status updates for the year 2017.

· Donald Trump has ~~just~~ ~~just~~ just become an official president of ~~At~~ the USA. What were people thinking. ~~#~~ get him impeached

· There was an extremist attack on London Bridge ~~or~~ if you didn't already know and I hope everyone feeling grief is doing ok. It will get better - I promise

· Women can now join all roles in the R.A.F. This is very overdue. I hope this means more gender equality for England.

You are an astronaut. Describe your perfect day.

(on Earth, in my own city)

It was 6am, I woke up early to see the sunrise. A shiny silver lever gleamed in the darkness (it was supposed to) I pulled it. And Suddenly, harsh white lights slowly lit up the thick darkness. Now I could see every single button or lever for all the different things I have to be in control of. My eyes burnt with the sudden brightness that seemed to echo of the walls It was worse when I first started out on the ship.

I swam through chilly air reaching for the observation room. With The windows revealed the globe and I saw deep blue and green mingle with white as the far sun gave it's light warming the Earth in the morning light It was day for some places but where it rose now was the most beautiful and easily seen Sunrise.

A few hours later, it was time for my meeting with TNESS (the national English Space Station) The meeting went really well. I'm coming home in a few weeks and the ship is in a fine condition.

In the evening, I finally was allowed my monthly talk with my family. Seeing them felt like seeing a puppy for the first time as a baby. I love them so much and I'll stay on course with the space walk tomorrow so I can see them as soon as possible.

Tell a story that begins with a ransom note.

'You're probably missing your little boy right now. I'm afraid you won't get him back unless I see £1,000,000 more in my bank account because I know you've got it.' That was all the note said. I'd read it sixteen times now looking for clues. My heart dropped like a pheasant that had been shot. My heart raced like Usain Bolt. Everything had changed. What could I do? I hardly even knew where I was anymore. The words seemed to leap off the page taunting me in my terror. It was a dream. It was a dream. Or was it?

The detective stared at me. It seemed she was waiting for me to tell her where my brother was. My mum and dad were too distraught to help. Therefore, it was all on me to help the police find my brother. It had already been three weeks and my parents barely left their room anymore. A red address s address tauntingly stood out. Even though we'd already checked there. It was a dingy room with thin walls dripping with rain. Darkness enveloped every corner and coated every object in the room. Surprisingly, one light spread a warm glow over a ballot box that read had 'place the money here' engraved upon the black plastic store.

I was also beginning to believe my brother would never return. Cold rivers of tears trickled down my worry free. Could we ever have £1,000,000 to give?

Something you had that was stolen

A while ago, I had a little blue notebook. It had gold detailing covered in a thick coat of dew. I'd left it out overnight and it was slightly wet. This was the day I lost my notes from the post. I have been writing in it for about 3 years now. It's 5cm thick. My friend didn't like it at all and one day it went missing. He left the same day. I can only steal one thing. What are the chances? What are the chances?! I think

The long-lost roommate

Once, before university I had a mini little flat. It was rather gnarled and ancient. A chilly draft always seemed to whisper in your ear. A layer of dust inevitably constantly covered the curtains. When you close them, the dust goes down your thought and makes you choke. I had a roommate named Naomi and she was kind but rather elusive. She had long, brown locks and eyes like a summer sky. However, one night she never came back. I'd seen her go to her university but she never returned. I left a few days later.

What a character holding a blue object is thinking right now

My head swirled. I didn't know what would happen but I guess I've found out. I held the pillow in my arms like it was the crown jewels. I probably felt as if I was coloring the rings on my nose. Although I knew I'd be fine but did I ?! It was re terrifying. but I knew I'd be ok but that I saw my family and for sister's friends staring at me with solemn apprehension.

Write a scene where the only spoken dialogue is "Uh-huh," "Umm," "Urrrr," "Mm-mmm."

Tell a complete stranger about a beloved family tradition.

You have just swallowed your pride and done something you didn't want
to do. Your friend wants to know why. The two of you are driving around
an almost-full parking garage looking for a space for the friend's
oversize pickup. Write the scene.

Pick a small object to be given one day to your great-grandchild.
Write a letter to that child explaining why you have chosen this object.

Describe yourself in the third person—your physical appearance
and personality—as though you were a character in a book.

Describe something you wanted badly and, once you got it, never used.

Describe an electronic device in the future that you won't know how to operate.

A storm destroys your uncle's shed and kills his six-year-old son. Describe the color of the sky right before the storm hit.

Name the trees that stood in the neighborhood where you grew up.

Write a scene in which a woman is fired after only a week on the job.
Just a week earlier, the same person who is now firing her was very
persuasive in convincing her to take the job.

Write a short story that is set in Argentina in 1932,
in which a teacup plays a crucial role.

Describe the most recent moment when you couldn't think of anything to say. Were you having a hard time making conversation, or were you simply dumbfounded?

What could have happened to you in high school that would have altered the course of your life?

You are looking down through the skylight as chefs prepare dinner
for your ex-fiancé's wedding.

Put two people who hate each other in an elevator for 12 hours.
What happens?

Something you lost

Something you found

A sneeze

The meanest thing anyone
has ever said to you

Describe five memories—events you remember really well.
Then take one of them further.

A man jumps from the fortieth story of a building. As he's passing the twenty-eighth floor, he hears a phone ring and regrets that he jumped. Why?

Write a recipe for disaster.

Your friend calls to say she saw you in the back
of a police car yesterday. What happened?

Tell the true story of a dramatic moment in your life,
but weave in one secret and one lie.

A cockroach at the Roosevelt

How you feel about love these days

The talk-show host

If you had one week to live . . .

The next blockbuster medicine that will be invented and what
will happen as a result

If each decade of your life was
represented by a pop song,
what would they be?

Describe each person in your family
with just one word.

What you would run out of the house
with if your house caught on fire

Something you've always
regretted saying

Write a scene that begins: "Joe was the last person on Earth
I expected to do that."

The thoughts of the first man to eat an oyster

Your most transcendent ice cream experience

Describe exultation.

The time you were the most terrified—your knees were knocking, your
heart was racing, you could barely stand to be in your own skin

---

The difference between the first death you remember
and the most recent one

Write a review of a novel or memoir you've never written.

I didn't know what was happening at the time.

Your city one hundred years from now

Write a short story in which you are the villain.

A bad situation that turned
out for the best

Finding a bag of cash

Would you rather win the Nobel Prize
or be a rock star?

Thoughts on your favorite
pet's personality

The moment you knew you were no longer a child

The worst thing that could happen

The best thing that could happen

Write a short story that is set in Detroit in 1956,
in which a car floor mat plays a crucial role.

A woman thinks she might be living next door to her grandson.

A man giving a speech to a crowd of thousands is suddenly caught
in a bald-faced lie.

What a character wearing something red is thinking

Your favorite moment in film

The menu for your last meal

Choose how you will die.

What would you be doing if you weren't doing this?

Write, in ridiculous detail, directions on how to get to your house.

A useless love—a connection or affinity that doesn't fit into
the plans of anyone concerned

You are a midlevel Greek deity, hoping to move up the ranks
of Olympus. What are your powers, and how will you use them to
impress Zeus and the others?

List five cultural events that impacted you greatly.
Then write about one of them without mentioning yourself.

Pick a person, then ask yourself: What is the hardest choice
this person has ever had to make?

You've just realized that you've lost something valuable in a
nightclub (a necklace, a wallet, a phone). What happens next?

The greatness of sandwiches

Parades

Boxers or briefs? Discuss.

Screw you.

Write about a difficult conversation you've had recently. Then rewrite
the conversation, saying what you couldn't say at the time.

Write the copy for a cereal box so that someone would actually
want to buy this exciting new flavor.

The cleaning lady

Waiting

An estranged mother and son who haven't seen or spoken to each other
in more than twenty years meet in line at the post office in December,
arms full of packages to be mailed. What do they say to each other?

Write a scene that begins: "It was the first time I killed a man."

Write a scene in which a person is leaving a restaurant with her
husband and bumps into a former lover. What words are exchanged or
not exchanged? What do her body positions say?

Go out to dinner with a friend, and as soon as you get home, write
in that person's voice. Begin with something the person said.

The president's personal to-do list

The general manager of the New York Yankees' personal to-do list

A powerful Hollywood agent's personal to-do list

Three objects in your
childhood bedroom

The toy you most treasured

What's stored in your closet?

The next sound you hear
and what caused it

Pick a country, and imagine we've been at war with it for fourteen years.
Write a love story set in that world.

A soldier is about to embark upon a mission that she
knows will kill her.

Write from the perspective of a historical figure like
Franklin Roosevelt, Marilyn Monroe, or Jack the Ripper.

Describe your favorite part of a man's body using only verbs.

Describe your favorite part of a woman's body using only verbs.

There are often three reasons for something: the reason we tell others, the reason we tell ourselves, and the real reason. Write about the war among the three.

You're having lunch with a friend. Your friend gets a call in the middle of the meal. Write just your friend's part of the conversation.

Describe one of your bad habits and why you secretly get joy out of it.

A child needs to do one thing over and over to calm himself down when the adults get angry. What does he do? How did he learn it?

Start a story with the line "When I confronted him,
he denied that he'd ever said it."

A newly invented product that
will change your life

A tree from the point of view
of one of its leaves

What nobody ever said to you

The car your father drove

Your bedroom from the point of view of a stranger
forced to occupy it for a week

You are a private investigator. You've been following a cheating husband
for a month. Write the report to your client—an emotionally unstable
wife—telling her what you did and what you've learned.

You wake up by the side of the road lying next to a bicycle,
with no memory and no wallet. What happens in the next hour?

Write a story that starts with a piece of gossip.

What your desk thinks about at night

A kid in your grade whom you don't know very well shows up at
your house one day to tell you something important. What does
he look like? What does he say?

What you would shoplift

Her secret obsession

You bring someone back
from the dead. Who is it?

You get to be any singer you choose
and sing one song in a live concert.

Write stage directions for an actor that insult him or
her personally all along the way.

The first time you were worried that you had come off sounding racist

Think of an object that describes you. Describe it.

Make a case for your favorite fruit.

Do a detailed character sketch for a fictional character about whom you would never, ever want to write. Work to avoid making up anything that would capture your own interest.

Write an anonymous letter to a stranger detailing
the things you've learned about life.

An e-mail that you inadvertently sent to someone who
wasn't supposed to see it

The most troubling phone call you hope you never receive

Set something on fire.

What is the place or object from your childhood that you most
think about when you think about home?

Describe a room in your house.

The first lie you were caught in

Where you wish you were

The carpenter who brought candy

Your favorite piece of
playground equipment

You track down an old boyfriend/girlfriend.

You realize you have inadvertently become a stalker.

You have a dream that you've murdered someone. Who is it, how
and why did the murder happen, and what happens afterward?

Ten years from now, you meet up with an old friend you haven't
seen in a decade. Write the conversation you have.

The person in your life you're most jealous of

You are a serial killer. What TV shows are on your DVR list? Why?

The one thing you're most ashamed of

A guilty pleasure

Comfort

Honesty

What you've kept

Who people think you are, compared to who you know you are

Find a section of your writing that has no energy to it and rewrite it
as one long sentence. Be sure that the sentence keeps expanding outward,
don't worry about it being a run-on, and just let it flow.

Put two characters, each of whom wants something from the other, in a room together. Neither of them is allowed to ask for it straight out. Give them five minutes with only dialogue to get what they want.

Write two prayers for your character: one to be said in private,
one to be said in public.

You are lost in a foreign country. You can't find anyone who
speaks English. How do you react, and how do you find your way?

Make a scene with a character exhibiting really bad behavior.

What you used to do that you don't do anymore

The people who will live in your house after you move out

The corpse you saw in the undertaker's window

Write down the names of a person who haunts you from the grave,
a person who fascinates you, and a person you don't understand.
Put them together in a scene.

The kill fee

Your favorite wine

That person your mother
always warned you about

Irresistible temptation

Start a story with: "This is what she wants most in the world."

_____
_____
_____
_____
_____
_____
_____
_____
_____

After the above prompt, try this:
"She is lying. _This_ is what she wants most in the world."

_____
_____
_____
_____
_____
_____
_____
_____
_____
_____

Find a short story you haven't yet read. Read the first two-thirds.
Then pick up the story where it leaves off, and write its end.

Finish the sentence that begins "What I've always wanted to say is . . ."

What would you buy from the *SkyMall* catalog? Why?

What does writer's block feel like?

Find a world map or globe, close your eyes, pick a spot. Write about
a person arriving there for the first time.

What you were doing this
time last year

An unexpected gift

Set your alarm for 3 a.m., wake up,
and write the first thing
that comes to mind.

Introduce your long-time
imaginary friend.

Open your kitchen cabinet. Write a scene incorporating the
first three things you see.

You are Frankenstein. Write a letter to Mary Shelley thanking
her for making your story known.

Write a short obituary of a stranger you've recently encountered. Then
rewrite it from the point of view of the person's estranged child.

Find a photograph. Write the story of what's happening outside the frame.

Remember something momentous that happened to you.
Then write about what happened right before the incident.

Write about an arrival that caught you or your character
completely unaware.

Explain to the historians of 2150 what it's like to go to a
shopping mall. Remember that they may not have malls in 2150.
Or escalators, food courts, or cash.

Begin a letter: "I am telling you this story because you are the only person who will not judge me . . ."

Write a scene full of sound and fury, signifying nothing.

Things you should throw away but can't

Describe a professor coming on to one of his students.

Your favorite hiding place

Something more you'd like
to know about

The way the sky looks today

A present from your mother

Write down three pieces of dialogue that you hear from
three different conversations. Put those bits into the
same conversation. Take it from there.

One day a young boy climbs a tree and decides he won't come down
until his parents stop their divorce proceedings. Write about the
event from the point of view of each parent.

Rewrite your college application essay from today's point of
view, answering the last question: "Is there anything else we
should know?"

Google search your own name. Write about the search result
that is the closest to your name but isn't you.

Describe one physical change you would make to yourself if you could and how this would change your life.

_____

_____

_____

_____

_____

_____

_____

_____

You are a customer lying face down on the floor during a bank robbery. Describe the robbery from this vantage point.

_____

_____

_____

_____

_____

_____

_____

_____

_____

Your favorite film

Your favorite book

Your favorite quote

Your favorite tree

Study a stranger. Go home and write a tragedy about his or her mother.

How you're just like your mother

Making soup

Write a paragraph in a language of your own invention.

Pick one decision you've made in your life—a move, job, or relationship. How would your life be different now if you'd made a different choice?

What did you wear to prom? How did you get your outfit, and what happened to it?

Three people (one might be you) at three ages looking at
things they shouldn't be looking at

Write a "Dear John" letter, breaking up with your high-school
sweetheart who's in the army.

You're the high school sweetheart from the above prompt. Write
your reply to the breakup note.

What was the most recent incident in your life that made you upset?

What was the most recent incident in your life that made you laugh?

Describe your best friend.

A bad smell and where it came from

The last thing you'd want to do

The nape of her husband's neck

Your most treasured photograph

Write a sex scene you wouldn't show your mom.

Rewrite the sex scene from above into one that you'd let your mom read.

Write a life as a series of postcards.

Five things you wish your mother had never told you

Describe Heaven.

Write a stand-up comedy routine to address the United Nations.

Something you never told your mother

A missing body part

A piece of clothing you keep
just for the memory

The oldest item in
your possession

Go outside and notice three distinct sounds. Remove the labels
and describe exactly what they sound like. Then write a story
incorporating the sounds.

It's 2100 and the world is running out of fresh water.
Describe a typical day.

You wake up in an open field wearing an astronaut suit
and lying on a surfboard. What happened?

The secret that, if revealed, would upset everything

Be your character's fortune teller. Tell his or her future.

Your dog's last dream

Write a story using four *L* words: lipstick, lust, loss, locked.

Write from the point of view of a literary character who changed your life.

A vivid childhood memory from the child's perspective

Write a survival guide for a character:
Ten things to do in an emergency.

You're the White House head chef, preparing a state dinner for the president of India. What do you serve, and how does it turn out?

Your favorite TV newscaster's hair

Where will you be exactly one year
from this moment?

Your favorite jeans

The last time you cheated

The orchestra on the *Titanic* famously kept playing as the ship went down.
Describe the sinking of the *Titanic* from the point of view of the musicians
playing in the ballroom—from their interactions to the sights, sounds, and
sensations they experience as the ship sinks.

You are stuck on the highway in the world's worst
traffic jam for at least two days. What happens?

Describe a trip to an amusement park, focusing on the colors,
sounds, smells, and tastes of the day.

You're confined to your bed for three months due to a serious
illness. What do you miss, and what's the first thing you'll do
once they let you outside?

Write for 10 minutes about what is running through a husband-to-be's
head while his wife-to-be is walking down the aisle to the altar where
he stands.

You can keep only one memory from
your entire life. What will it be?

The art of love

What you ate for breakfast

Toto, if we're not in Kansas
anymore, where are we?

Tell the story of a time you lost an argument.

Write a love letter to a person you dislike.

Write a story that ends with the line
"And this is the room where it happened."

What won't you touch with a 10-foot pole? Why?

A strange girl who hides herself under layers and layers of clothing

---

Five things you wish you'd asked your grandmother or grandfather

You are the pilot of a jumbo jet, just realizing the plane may
crash. What will you tell the crew and the passengers?

It's your first day on Death Row. Plan the next ten years of your
life in this eight-by-ten cell, as you wait for your day to come.

What was the last thing you cared about that you misplaced? Write about what happened, with as many sentences as possible in the active voice. ("I forgot my cell. I looked under the couch. I called a friend.")

Rewrite the description from above in the passive voice—whereby no one does anything. ("My cell was forgotten. Lint was the only thing that the couch had to offer. A call to my friend went nowhere.")

Imagine a character at two very different ages,
and describe his or her day at each age.

_____

_____

_____

_____

_____

_____

_____

_____

_____

_____

_____

_____

_____

_____

_____

_____

_____

_____

_____

_____

_____

Going it alone

A moment of forgiveness

Tell the world's saddest joke.

Everyone has a special talent.
What's your special skill?

Describe your mother.

_____

_____

_____

_____

_____

_____

Five ideas for a novel that you'll never write

_____

_____

_____

_____

_____

_____

What did you dream about last night?

_____

_____

_____

_____

_____

_____

You are the lawyer in a divorce case. The only point of contention
is custody of the dog. Argue that your client should get the pup.

You are living in Atlanta in 1864. Atlanta is burning.
What do you do?

Write two descriptions of yourself for an online dating service. First,
be the kind of guy/girl who'd be taken home to meet the mother. Then
try a hot, sexy version.

What is your favorite line or passage from a book, movie,
play, or poem? Try writing your own versions of this line.

Go to the Merriam-Webster Word of the Day Web site (www.merriam-webster.com/word-of-the-day), and write a story based on that word.

Your worst experience
on an airplane

Your best birthday

A recipe for beat(nik) soup

List the ways in which
you fight life.

Describe the face of someone you love.

A boy who tries to be funny when nobody is
laughing at his jokes

Something goes wrong at your favorite camping spot.

Alfred Hitchcock said that a mystery is not knowing what will happen to a bunch of guys playing poker; suspense is when only you know there's a bomb underneath the poker table. Write about a banal event, but start by introducing something that will change everything and that only the reader knows is coming.

A four-year-old child is afraid of the dark. Write about the child's fears and what you might say or do to help the child overcome the fears.

You, a grown adult, are afraid of the dark. Explain why this is a legitimate concern, so friends won't laugh at you.

Write a single paragraph that conveys a lot about a character's life.
Think about how this can be achieved with voice and rhythm and repetition.

What is the sound of silence, and when did you last hear it?
What was missing?

You have been evicted from your home, but rather than live on the
street you go to Ikea. At night you hide in the bathroom until the
janitor leaves. Write about your life.

Think of an episode from your life that you don't dare write.
Write it.

Keep a list of words you like, for their sound, for their meaning,
or just for their goofy spelling. Pick one of those words and use
it in a paragraph.

A dream your boss had

A family (not your own) on the
street where you grew up

The way you mistreated a friend

A letter to the editor

Write your own *Back to the Future* moment: Describe how your parents
met and how those tiny details set the stage for their relationship
and your existence.

Go to a café and closely watch two people interact.
Then write a scene about two people in a café.

At a romantic restaurant on a busy Saturday night, a guy gets down
on one knee and begins to propose. You are a sportscaster doing
color commentary of the occasion for a live television audience.

Five things that always get you into trouble

Another drunken episode

You are a fifty-three-year-old woman living in Chicago.
Write a letter to Santa.

Even a broken clock is right twice a day. Give some good advice
from a completely unreliable source, and convince someone to
take this advice.

Write about a song

Describe nearly drowning.

The thirty-year lie

Two dollars isn't a lot
of money, unless . . .

Describe *ascent* using the most innovative, outrageous metaphors, similes, and physical descriptions you can think of.

What does your sleeping, dreaming mind think in the moments before you wake up? What are its last hopes, fears, or promises to itself as the alarm goes off and it feels itself vanishing?

You've had a really rotten day, you're mad at the world, and in an evil moment you decide to give a classroom full of impressionable, hopeful young writers all the worst possible advice anyone could give . . .

You wake up with a nameless feeling of dread in your gut, but you can't figure out what it is. Write down everything that could possibly happen during the day that could be something for you to dread.

Your most embarrassing moment

The weekend in St. Tropez

Write a letter from a coach to a parent of a player,
explaining why the player quit the team.

Write a scene in which the protagonist is wrongly accused of
conspiring to cause a big accident.

You are a camp counselor. Make up a story that will scare the
bejeezus out of your eight- to ten-year-old campers.

What you really wanted to say to the customer service representative
when you called about your broken appliance

The perfect crime—and what could go wrong

A day in the life of the person sitting next to you

The kleptomaniac

The point of view
of a blind person

A never-ending breakup

A death in the family

Your character is swimming in a lake, not wearing her glasses.
She squints at a shape coming toward her in the water. What
does she think she sees?

Your grandmother gave you a book that you refuse to read.
What's the book? Write a thank-you note to your grandmother,
pretending that you read it.

Write a love scene from the point of view of your hands.

A woman is struggling to get a large package into the trunk
of her car. Her son doesn't get out of the car to help her.
Write the scene.

Write your will, explaining who gets what and your changes of
mind over the years about it.

Think of a person you despise. Now describe all the wonderful
things about that person.

How someone saved your life

You find your great-great-grandmother's diary.
On June 16, 1856, she wrote:

A beginner's guide to
getting noticed

Tenth anniversary

Being chased by a killer

On becoming a tycoon

Write a press release announcing the biggest moment in your life. Pitch why this event is of interest to the masses and the reporters who will decide whether to cover it.

Write a music review for the sounds of your life—your
personal, everyday soundtrack.

Pick your most cherished political view and convincingly
argue the other side.

How your cat sees the world

Everyone was laughing, except you.

Write a poem about a tomato.

You are going to appear on a talk show. The producer comes backstage to elicit a funny story that the host should focus on. Write the story like a monologue you're giving on national TV.

_____

_____

_____

_____

_____

_____

_____

_____

_____

_____

_____

_____

_____

_____

_____

_____

_____

_____

_____

_____

Write a story based on the title of your favorite song.

Write about a time someone completely screwed you over. Endeavor to
convince the reader that you were entirely blameless in the events.

....

....

....

....

....

....

....

....

....

Write about the same event from the above prompt with the intent of
convincing the reader that you were fully to blame. Which version
of the story is more convincing?

....

....

....

....

....

....

....

....

....

....

Describe the biggest earthquake
you've ever heard about.

Link two encounters from your day.

An hour to go

Death of a journalist

Describe an experience from the point of view of someone who is phobic about that very experience. For example, an airplane flight taken by someone terrified of flying, an agoraphobic lost in a pasture, an arachibutyrophobic eating a sandwich.

Write down the interior monologue you experience
when you sit down to write.

Each member of the San Francisco Giants can request the song
that will be playing when he goes up to bat. Write the lyrics
to the song that would be playing when you are up to bat.

You walk into your bedroom and discover someone going though your drawers.

You know the person with whom you're talking is lying.
Do you confront him or let him continue?

There are two kinds of people: drunks and survivors of drunks.
Which are you?

Pick a classic fairy tale, and set it in your modern-day hometown.

The biggest lie anyone told you

A tour of Jamaica

How to get rich quick

Arsenic

You are a thirteen-year-old. Write a love letter to your boyfriend.

You are twenty-one-year-old. Write a love letter to your girlfriend.

Where would you be now if you had married your first love?

....

....

....

....

....

....

Imagine someone who tells a lie to himself and others.
What would happen if he stopped?

....

....

....

....

....

....

Put your character (or yourself) in the dark. See what happens.

....

....

....

....

....

....

You are a military officer responsible for going to people's homes to tell
them that a family member has died in combat, is a prisoner of war, injured,
missing in action, and the like. Describe one of the notification scenes.

Two paramedics have a patient in the back of the ambulance. The patient has only about 30 minutes to live. It could take 20 minutes or more to get to the hospital. What's going on in the ambulance?

You'd just die if anyone ever saw this diary entry.

You have a time machine, but it can only go back in time two days. What would you change?

Write from this quote from Claude Lévi-Strauss, "I am the
place in which something has occurred."

You're a Nigerian e-mail scammer. Write an e-mail that will
convince the recipient to send you $200.

A person is standing on a soapbox in the park, yelling at
passersby. What's going on?

The smell of a
place you love

What you ate for breakfast

Pregnant and lost

Getting hit by lightning

You have just been caught in bed by a jealous spouse.
How will you talk your way out of this?

Take one aspect of routine life—such as grocery shopping or
putting gas in the car—and remove it. What happens when a
character stops doing that? Why would he do so?

Columbus sailed the ocean blue in 1492. Write some other short rhymes or mnemonics about historic events or important facts that a schoolkid might have to learn.

Time magazine has just named you "Person of the Year." Why?

It's a big, raucous house party of drunken high-school students. Describe the scene in three ways: as one of the teens attending the party, as the police officer called to the scene, and as a parent of one of the teens.

Write an acceptance speech for your party's nominee for governor.

Justify the one thing in your life you know you should be rid
of but you just can't bear to give up.

What ten questions are you going to ask to figure out the object
in a game of I Spy?

Just when I thought I knew what
she'd say next . . .

Finding a bone in a parking lot

The fortune teller in the window

Death is like this . . .

Write a sermon for a beloved preacher who has been caught in a sex scandal.

You've been caught cheating at a casino. Explain to the pit
boss why this is all just a big misunderstanding.

What is your shrink really thinking when you tell him about
your day, your life, your hopes, your fears?

Spin around until you get so dizzy you fall down. Write about
the first thought that comes into your head.

Pick your favorite movie. Now switch the sex of the lead.
Adjust the plot accordingly.

Write about something you know absolutely nothing about.
Make all of it up.

Polite dinner conversation isn't supposed to include religion, politics, or money. Write a scene at the dinner table where one or more of these topics is discussed.

Write the lyrics of a catchy jingle—for a plumbing service.

_____

_____

_____

_____

_____

_____

Write down everything you can remember about your algebra teacher.

_____

_____

_____

_____

_____

_____

Never underestimate the lives of old men sitting on park benches.

_____

_____

_____

_____

_____

_____

You're filling a time capsule to bury in the backyard that will be dug up in five hundred years. Write the letter you'd put inside to describe life as you know it today.

Write a life as the inventory of an auction.

Why your boss should
give you a raise

How the other half lives

A road to hell paved with
good intentions

Your first time in a
foreign country

Describe a mortician's meeting with a newly bereaved family. Remember that he isn't just dealing with grief but selling a funeral package and getting necessary information about the deceased and the survivors.

Write wedding vows. The bride is thirty-five years old; it's her first marriage. The groom is forty-eight, and it's his third go-round at the altar.

Pick a dictator and write about an imaginary morning or day of
his life, focusing on the banalities (digestion, sleep, oral
hygiene).

The person you loved who didn't love you back

Write a music review that doesn't refer to any other bands,
musicians, or genres, but can refer to anything else.

Describe a time when you wanted to orgasm but couldn't.

Approach a stranger, introduce yourself, and ask him or her to tell you
something he or she has never told anyone else. Record your findings.

Why you write

That day in Paris

What people don't
understand about you

Your first fight

Put yourself or your character in a place where you feel
vulnerable and uneasy.

The apology a recently disgraced public figure should have
offered up, in place of the one penned by his or her public
relations handlers

Watch a group of people do exactly the same thing—board a subway car and look for a seat, for example. Describe each individual in a sentence or two, using a different verb in each sentence.

Suddenly, you can hear everyone's thoughts, and you are shocked by what they think about you. Write their thoughts.

Begin a story describing only two hands. Use the physical characteristics of
the hands, as well as any relevant activity or movement, gesture, fidgeting,
and so on, to reveal who the hands belong to.

Fix the plot of the worst movie you've ever seen.

Write the lyrics of a rap song. They must include a cop, a
bad drug bust, and a dog.

A child is doing homework with an adult. Who are they? Reveal
their relationship through their interaction about the schoolwork.

Elvis Costello said that writing about music is like dancing
about architecture. Discuss.

Interview someone you admire. Write a short profile of the person.

The last time you changed your mind about something important

Your worst experience during
a family dinner

Your worst experience
in a bar

Your worst experience
playing a sport

Your worst experience
in gym class

Turn to the obituaries section of the newspaper, and choose one person
to write about. Imagine a scene in that person's life.

Write about a vivid but troubled figure from literature as if he or she were
your grandparent or great-grandparent. Look for the ways their lives reveal
the patterns of codependency, addiction, avoidance, or whatever else you're
dealing with in your own family.

You are Bill Gates, and you are trying to solve the world's problems one at a time. What's the first thing you are going to tackle? Why?

Write a list of things to do before you die.

My grandfather's girlfriend

Describe a moment in which you were in physical pain.

Describe an item of clothing you wear now that someday your son or daughter will want to own. What is it, and why will your child want to wear it in twenty years?

Staying at the Harvard Club

An ethical dilemma

Describe a person you
see every day.

Describe a person you've
never met.

Ethan Canin said that he wrote "The Accountant" (in *The Palace Thief*) because he wanted to write a story in which a pair of socks seemed important. Pick an ordinary object. Make it someone's obsession. Write a story about the obsession.

You are a radio disc jockey who has been handed a news alert about an explosion downtown. People are to evacuate the area. What do you say or do on air as further information does (or does not) come into the station?

Why is it true that you are right so much of the time and everyone else gets things so wrong?

Write about the scene at The Kasino Club, the only bar in Stanley, Idaho, on an ordinary Tuesday night. Stanley's population is just under five hundred, and it's best known for being the coldest place in the lower forty-eight.

You are a loser who lives alone with a cat and have for quite some time. One day your cat can't take it anymore and starts talking. What does it say?

You are in a department store in another city, and you see one of your teachers weeping. Write the scene.

Five things you see out the nearest window

Describe your favorite athlete.

Why do you like those shoes?

She was a fat woman whose eating habits were dainty. There was a check for $13,612 in her purse, not made out to her, but, you know. She was good at figuring these things out. Start with her hair.

The glow of success

Your dream vacation

The end of the world

Your last cry

I can't go into this right now, but if I could, I'd tell you this . . .

Re-create your earliest childhood memory.

Write a scene where a couple get into the biggest argument of their marriage—in a small fishing boat, on their favorite lake, at dawn. The motor broke, and they're far out.

Explain what dentists do for a cavity. Your audience:
a six-year-old child with cavity-ridden teeth.

Do people still care about the common politic and culture?
Why or why not?

Your favorite recipe

A character discovers an object hidden many years ago in a family home.

Write a scene in which a father accidentally meets his son's girlfriend for the first time. The son isn't present, and the girlfriend is almost the same age as the father.

Rewrite a piece of your own writing
in one-syllable words.

Describe your grandmother's
childhood.

Ten bad bar pickup lines

Ten euphemisms for sex

The most recent time you were betrayed

Write a song.

Write a children's story set in the woods.

You are a brand-new suicide-hotline counselor. Describe how
you feel during the course of your first call.

_____

_____

_____

_____

_____

_____

Do you have a superstition? What is it, why do you have it,
and how do you follow it?

_____

_____

_____

_____

_____

_____

Explain to your boss why you spent $5,000 during one business
meeting and why he should reimburse you.

_____

_____

_____

_____

_____

_____

James Joyce said that a man's errors are his portals of discovery.
What mistakes have led to epiphanies for you?

Write a letter to a child explaining how to do one thing
(for example, ride a horse or throw a punch).

A translator doesn't want to translate what she's just been told.

Come up with every possible way to describe something as
"red," without using the word itself.

Write a script to give telemarketers to sell plastic
pooper-scoopers.

Write a script to give telemarketers to solicit donations
for starving children in Africa.

Life in a snowbound cabin

Life among the pirates

The way things should
have been

Write a letter to
your landlord.

A hopelessly messy person and an obsessively
neat person become roommates.

Write about two characters who have known each other for
a long time, and give one of them a secret.

A road trip with your sister

A conversation about you that you weren't supposed to overhear

A physical description of an eccentric relative

Wisdom you learned from your child

What you think about that always brings you to tears

Where do you go to escape?

Write about what you are worrying
about right now.

An elaborate and complicated lie

Your most memorable experience
in the back of a car

"Let's go, sugarbeet," he said and snapped on the light. He was
holding two duffle bags, one very light, the other very heavy. It
was her car, and she had slept with the keys.

Write a letter from the point of view of a drug addict.

Write a letter to the reader of a novel you haven't written yet.

A 24-hour camping trip with any person you want

A straight-A high-school student is caught stealing something at
school by a teacher.

Think of the most frightening experience anyone has ever related to you—
a carjacking, a dogfight, a robbery—and imagine what it must have been like
to be personally involved. Start with the experience in real time.

An argument at Sunday dinner

You're in the interview stage of the Miss America pageant. Besides your desire for world peace, what will you tell the judges?

What do you own that will be obsolete in twenty years?
What will replace it?

A conversation you regret never having

Through a freak illness, you lose one of your senses. Which sense is it, what happens to you, and how do you deal with it?

A beginner's guide to
complete satisfaction

A beginner's guide to winning
over your in-laws

A beginner's guide to getting
up in the morning

A beginner's guide to
skipping out of work

You know when it comes to a decision between the job that pays well and the
job that's fun? He made the colossal mistake of picking the fun job.

Put your iPod on random shuffle, write down the lyric of the
first song that comes on, and use it as an opening line.

Rewrite the Gettysburg Address for today's audience.

One of your parents has a habit that really annoys you.
What's the habit? Does anybody besides you notice it?

Describe the sounds you heard the first time you swam in the ocean.

If your brother knew you'd said that about him, he'd flay you
alive. What did you say?

Choose a family story for which you were not present. Choose the narrator of the piece (your mother, your older brother, your great-great-great aunt) and write the event in his or her voice.

What broke your heart

Waking up elsewhere

A lie you told and
got away with

Write a "bucket list" for
your favorite superhero.

You are the high-school valedictorian.
Write your valedictory address.

Take the bare facts from a court complaint or investigation at
ACLU.org and retell them as a full descriptive narrative.

Identify a powerful and significant personal experience from your past (the birth of a younger sibling, breaking your arm, a family road trip, divorce). Then change the setting, and write a story in which your narrator encounters that experience.

Imagine you were unable to speak for a year. What would you do to communicate, and what impact would it have on your relationships? What would you be saving up to say at the end of the year?

It was the first time he had ever gotten into a fight, and it was in a _____ of all places.

Rant about something you hate—let loose. Now rewrite that rant with the intention of convincing someone else to share your feelings.

Two guys walk into a bar . . .

A perfect meal

Create an imaginary friend (human or not).

You are a peasant in 1890s Russia. There is no food. Revolution is in the air.
The czarists offer meals for your allegiance. What do you do?

A rationalization
of bad behavior

Why you forgot to pay
your credit card bill

Describe in detail the most
boring thing imaginable.

Describe your last visit to a
doctor's office or hospital.

Write a "knock knock" joke. Then use it in a story.

Summarize your dog's life in fewer than four paragraphs.

Sit for 15 minutes in a tranquil place—the edge of a stream,
the courtyard of a church, an empty field—opening all your
senses. Write down what you notice.

Complete the following sentence and then keep writing:
"My first _____."

That time you peed your pants

Second marriage

Describe in detail an everyday object—a piece of fruit,
a water bottle, or your beat-up old wallet.

Start a story with the line "Everyone whispered about _____,
but no one had the courage to talk to her."

Imagine yourself at age eight.
What would you tell yourself?

Imagine yourself at age eighty.
What would you tell yourself?

What's the worst nightmare
you remember?

Write a bathroom
wall limerick.

What is public and what is private? What should be public and
what should be private? What do these terms mean now?

Describe your demographic group. Describe the stereotypes of your
group that you confirm. Describe the stereotypes you subvert.

Jot down some notes about a long-ago family event. Then interview
a family member about the event. Now write a piece featuring the
differences between the two memories.

Drink a beer. Write about the taste.

She was crazy that way.

Eavesdrop today—on the bus, in line for lunch, or on the
street. What do people say? What do they really sound like?

Interview a person you think you know well.
Ask questions you've never before asked.

Write about what you'll be worrying about five years from now.
Ten years from now. Thirty years from now.

Retell the most recent joke you've heard as a short piece of fiction.

Imagine an incident from your past in super-slow motion,
including your thoughts.

Write an X-rated Disney scenario.

Write a scathing review
of a classic book.

What is the worst thing
that you ever did?

What is the worst thing that
ever happened to you?

Extend a short interaction (e.g., paying for coffee, talking to a
phone operator) as long as possible.

Choose a person who interests you. Write about following the person home.

Write ten new cheers for a high-school cheerleading squad.

Begin writing with the following sentence: "That was the time
he stopped believing _____."

....

....

....

....

....

....

....

....

....

The last chapter of the relationship

....

....

....

....

....

....

....

....

....

The missing software engineer

I was not sorry.

A roomful of people who want to sleep together

Who wrote the Book of Love?
Why, and what's in it?

Write ten sayings for
fortune cookies.

Your day, hour by hour

A famous, unsolved crime

Start a story with the line "My mother broke every plate in the house that day."

It took her five million years to decide on a sandwich. But when _____
asked her to marry her, she knew the answer was yes. Her friends and family
said this was the wrong call. So here's how the whole mess played out . . .

You are Luke Skywalker. Write three different opening paragraphs
for your autobiography, trying out very different styles.

You are the Grim Reaper. Write three different opening paragraphs
for your autobiography, trying out very different styles.

Only ten people will fit in the life raft. Convince the captain
that you should be one of them.

Recall a recent dialogue between you and a friend.

Sitting in a single location for 20 minutes, take notes focusing
exclusively on the sounds you can hear.

Your last year on Earth

You've been stranded on an island for five years now.
Describe your typical day.

A scene that takes place
in extreme heat

A scene that takes place
in extreme cold

What is the most difficult decision
you've ever made?

Describe an eccentric
person in action.

Interview your oldest relative.

How is hand-held technology (i.e., cell phones, iPods) affecting public
social behavior and interaction in the public space? How has it impacted
everyday street life and our ability to meet and deal with strangers?

_____

_____

_____

_____

_____

_____

_____

_____

_____

_____

_____

_____

_____

_____

_____

_____

_____

_____

_____

Staying as close as possible to the tactile, be your character
having a skin allergy.

What's the most expensive thing you own?
What was it like to buy it?

Leaving home

Your face is on the evening news. Write a short news story to explain why.

Write a letter from a forty-five-year-old Lolita to an elderly
Humbert Humbert about the way he destroyed her childhood.

A time you made someone cry

A time someone made you cry

I have never felt this way
before or since . . .

The first summer you
fell in love

A kid throws a rock over a cliff, and it hits a man in the head. The kid
hears screams and goes to down to find the man's hiking partner, who reveals
that the man is dead. Write the conversation between the two.

Write a message in a bottle. Write about the person who finds it.

Begin with "It didn't seem like much at the time . . ."

Write from the point of view of a person who has synesthesia (a condition
in which one type of sensory stimulation evokes a different sense, as when
hearing a sound produces the visualization of a color).

The most painful letter you've ever had to write

You are a teenager. Your friend asks you to meet him at a culvert everyone knows isn't very safe. How do you get out of the house? What happens when you get there?

Describe an image that is embedded in your brain in detail and
why it remains there.

Write from the point of view of a nurse who hates the patient
she is charged with helping.

You are a superhero. What powers do you have, and how do you use them?

Start with "I never told anyone . . ."

Ten headlines you'd like to see in
the *New York Times* today and why

What happened that night

This is what _____'s life
looks like in public.

And this is what _____'s life
looks like in private.

Open with a bad joke.

Storyboard a comic.

Write a love letter to the one who got away.

Write a story from the point of view of a homeless man or woman who falls asleep on the bus and accidentally ends up "on the other side of the tracks," in a quiet neighborhood late at night.

_____

_____

_____

_____

_____

_____

_____

_____

_____

Rewrite the above story from the point of view of a wealthy stockbroker who ends up in the poorest part of town.

_____

_____

_____

_____

_____

_____

_____

_____

_____

_____

Open your medicine cabinet. Catalog every pill, ointment, and
product. What conditions do they treat and how does the whole
lot add up to a statement about your mortality?

Write a story in which each sentence will begin with a different
letter of the alphabet, beginning with the letter A, and moving
sequentially, i.e., B, C, D, and so forth.

A taste that excites you and the
moment you first encountered it

The first time you had sex

The poorest you've ever been

The richest you've ever been

Watch three spectators at a ball game and describe each one
as a different animal.

The most intriguing and/or unexpected conversation you've had
with a complete stranger

Write about something extraordinary in a flat voice.

Describe two visits to the circus from the point of view of someone who's bipolar. On one visit, he's manic, and on the other, he's in a pit of despair.

Write a scene in which two people leave believing opposite
things are true.

Scientists announce they've discovered the secret to immortality.
Write a petition letter to save the event of death.

Go to a new restaurant you've been dying to try. Enjoy your
meal. Go home and write a review as an undercover food critic.

Write down as many clichés and aphorisms as you can think of.
Go back, and star the ones you actually say.

Go through a day saying yes to every impulse and offer. If you
are not physically restrained, write about the experience and
where you end up.

Make up a Peanuts character. Write a scene in which your character
interacts with the other Peanuts characters.

Write down twenty details of your neighborhood block.

Write a scene set in a different location, using all the details from above.

Jot down a list of things
that make you angry.

Write about one thing on
the list to the left.

Losing your memory

How to get from point A to point B
. . . and why you might not want to

You are a contemporary Hollywood executive writing to James Joyce to suggest ways *Ulysses* could be made more "filmable." For example, add action sequences, create a happy ending, look for scenes that could use CGI special effects, suggest box-office names to play the roles and pop rock songs for the soundtrack.

Write the menu for a restaurant—including names for dishes and descriptions of flavors and ingredients. Then rewrite it for the delivery/to-go menu. The delivery menu must be half as long, but just as tantalizing.

You are a pirate. Describe your perfect day.

What's your biggest secret?
What would happen if it was just discovered?

_____

_____

_____

_____

_____

_____

_____

_____

_____

_____

The closest experience you've ever had to having your life
flash before your eyes

_____

_____

_____

_____

_____

_____

_____

_____

_____

Write an ode to an onion.

What's the stupidest thing you used to believe whole-heartedly?

That snappy reply you never had a chance to say

Go ahead. Judge a book by its cover. What does it look like?

Write a ransom note.

_____

_____

_____

_____

_____

_____

_____

_____

The best advice for a teen just graduating from high school

_____

_____

_____

_____

_____

_____

_____

_____

_____

_____

Share that embarrassing story your relatives always tell about you.

Pick a story from today's news. Imagine one of the people mentioned
in the article reading it at the breakfast table that same day.
Describe the scene.

Your first kiss

Your first breakup

You are happily married, but one day you realize you
have a crush on someone else. What happens?

Write your obituary.